IMPORTANT NOTES

Date: Day #

Location:

Today: ☺   ☺   ☹   ☹   ☹

Weather: ☀   ⛅   ☁   🌧   🌨

Notes

_____

_____

_____

_____

_____

_____

_____

_____

_____

_____

_____

_____

_____

_____

_____

_____

_____

_____

_____

_____

_____

_____

_____

_____

Date: Day #

Location:

Today: ☺   😐   🙁   🙁   😣

Weather: ☀   ⛅   ☁   🌧   🌨

Notes

_____

_____

_____

_____

_____

_____

_____

_____

_____

_____

_____

_____

_____

_____

_____

_____

_____

_____

_____

_____

_____

_____

_____

_____

_____

_____

Date: **Day #**

Location:

Today: 🙂   😐   🙁   😟   😣

Weather: ☀️   ⛅   ☁️   🌧️   🌨️

Notes

Date: Day #

Location:

Today: ☺   😐   ☹   😣   😠

Weather: ☀   ⛅   ☁   🌧   🌨

Notes

_____

_____

_____

_____

_____

_____

_____

_____

_____

_____

_____

_____

_____

_____

_____

_____

_____

_____

_____

_____

_____

_____

Date: Day #

Location:

Today: 🙂   😐   🙁   😣   😠

Weather: ☀️   ⛅   ☁️   🌧️   🌨️

Notes

_____

_____

_____

_____

_____

_____

_____

_____

_____

_____

_____

_____

_____

_____

_____

_____

_____

_____

_____

_____

_____

_____

_____

Date: Day #

Location:

Today: ☺   😐   🙁   ☹   😣

Weather: ☀   ⛅   ☁   🌧   🌨

Notes

_____

_____

_____

_____

_____

_____

_____

_____

_____

_____

_____

_____

_____

_____

_____

_____

_____

_____

_____

_____

_____

_____

Date: Day #

Location:

Today: ☺   ☺   ☹   ☹   ☹

Weather: ☀   ⛅   ☁   🌧   🌨

Notes

Date: _____   Day # _____

Location: _____

Today: 🙂   😐   🙁   😣   😠

Weather: ☀️   🌤️   ☁️   🌧️   🌨️

Notes

_____
_____
_____
_____
_____
_____
_____
_____
_____
_____
_____
_____
_____
_____
_____
_____
_____
_____
_____
_____
_____
_____
_____
_____
_____

Date: Day #

Location:

Today: 🙂   😐   🙁   ☹️   😣

Weather: ☀️   ⛅   ☁️   🌧️   🌨️

Notes

_____

_____

_____

_____

_____

_____

_____

_____

_____

_____

_____

_____

_____

_____

_____

_____

_____

_____

_____

_____

_____

_____

_____

_____

Date: **Day #**

Location:

Today: 🙂   😐   🙁   ☹️   😠

Weather: ☀️   ⛅   ☁️   🌧️   🌨️

Notes

Date: _____   Day #

Location: _____

Today: 😊   😐   🙁   ☹️   😣

Weather: ☀️   ⛅   ☁️   🌧️   🌨️

Notes

_____

_____

_____

_____

_____

_____

_____

_____

_____

_____

_____

_____

_____

_____

_____

_____

_____

_____

_____

_____

_____

_____

_____

_____

_____

Date: Day #

Location:

Today: ☺   😐   🙁   ☹   😣

Weather: ☀   ⛅   ☁   🌧   🌨

Notes

_____

_____

_____

_____

_____

_____

_____

_____

_____

_____

_____

_____

_____

_____

_____

_____

_____

_____

_____

_____

_____

_____

_____

Date: _____   Day #

Location: _____

Today: ☺   😐   🙁   😟   😣

Weather: ☀   ⛅   ☁   🌧   🌨

Notes

_____

_____

_____

_____

_____

_____

_____

_____

_____

_____

_____

_____

_____

_____

_____

_____

_____

_____

_____

_____

_____

_____

_____

_____

Date: Day #

Location:
Today: ☺   😐   🙁   😞   😣
Weather: ☀   ⛅   ☁   🌧   🌨

Notes

_____
_____
_____
_____
_____
_____
_____
_____
_____
_____
_____
_____
_____
_____
_____
_____
_____
_____
_____
_____
_____
_____
_____
_____
_____

Date: Day #

Location:

Today: ☺   😐   🙁   🙁   😣

Weather: ☀   ⛅   ☁   🌧   🌨

Notes

_____

_____

_____

_____

_____

_____

_____

_____

_____

_____

_____

_____

_____

_____

_____

_____

_____

_____

_____

_____

_____

_____

_____

_____

_____

Date: _____   Day #

Location: _____

Today: ☺ 😐 🙁 😟 😠

Weather: ☀ ⛅ ☁ 🌧 🌨

Notes

_____

_____

_____

_____

_____

_____

_____

_____

_____

_____

_____

_____

_____

_____

_____

_____

_____

_____

_____

_____

_____

_____

_____

_____

_____

Date: Day #

Location:

Today: ☺   😐   🙁   ☹   😣

Weather: ☀   ⛅   ☁   🌧   🌨

Notes

_____

_____

_____

_____

_____

_____

_____

_____

_____

_____

_____

_____

_____

_____

_____

_____

_____

_____

_____

_____

_____

_____

_____

_____

Date: _____   Day #

Location: _____

Today: 😊   😐   🙁   ☹️   😣

Weather: ☀️   ⛅   ☁️   🌧️   🌨️

Notes

_____
_____
_____
_____
_____
_____
_____
_____
_____
_____
_____
_____
_____
_____
_____
_____
_____
_____
_____
_____
_____
_____
_____
_____
_____
_____
_____

Date: Day #

Location:

Today: ☺   😐   ☹   😫   😣

Weather: ☀   ⛅   ☁   🌧   🌨

Notes

_____

_____

_____

_____

_____

_____

_____

_____

_____

_____

_____

_____

_____

_____

_____

_____

_____

_____

_____

_____

_____

_____

_____

_____

Date: Day #

Location:

Today: ☺   ☹   ☹   ☹   ☹

Weather: ☀   ⛅   ☁   🌧   🌨

Notes

Date: Day #

Location:

Today: :)   :| :(:((>:(

Weather: ☀   ⛅   ☁   🌧   🌨

Notes

_____

_____

_____

_____

_____

_____

_____

_____

_____

_____

_____

_____

_____

_____

_____

_____

_____

_____

_____

_____

_____

_____

_____

Date: Day #

Location:

Today: ☺   ☹   ☹   ☹   ☹

Weather: ☀   ⛅   ☁   🌧   🌨

Notes

Date: Day #

Location:

Today: ☺   ☺   ☹   ☹   ☹

Weather: ☀   ⛅   ☁   🌧   🌨

Notes

Date: Day #

Location:

Today: ☺   😐   ☹   😟   😣

Weather: ☀   ⛅   ☁   🌧   🌨

Notes

_____

_____

_____

_____

_____

_____

_____

_____

_____

_____

_____

_____

_____

_____

_____

_____

_____

_____

_____

_____

_____

_____

_____

_____

_____

Date: **Day #**

Location:

Today: ☺   😐   ☹   😖   😠

Weather: ☀   ⛅   ☁   🌧   🌨

Notes

_____

_____

_____

_____

_____

_____

_____

_____

_____

_____

_____

_____

_____

_____

_____

_____

_____

_____

_____

_____

_____

_____

_____

_____

Date: Day #

Location:

Today: ☺   😐   ☹   😟   😠

Weather: ☀   ⛅   ☁   🌧   🌨

Notes

Date: **Day #**

Location:

Today: ☺   😐   ☹   😧   😠

Weather: ☀   ⛅   ☁   🌧   🌨

Notes

Date: _____   Day #

Location: _____

Today: ☺   😐   ☹   😧   😠

Weather: ☀   ⛅   ☁   🌧   🌨

Notes

_____

_____

_____

_____

_____

_____

_____

_____

_____

_____

_____

_____

_____

_____

_____

_____

_____

_____

_____

_____

_____

_____

_____

_____

_____

_____

Date: Day #

Location:

Today: ☺   😐   ☹   😣   😠

Weather: ☀   ⛅   ☁   🌧   🌨

Notes

Date: Day #

Location:

Today: ☺   😐   ☹   😣   😠

Weather: ☀   ⛅   ☁   🌧   🌨

Notes

Date: Day #

Location:

Today: 🙂   😐   🙁   ☹️   😠

Weather: ☀️   ⛅   ☁️   🌧️   🌨️

Notes

_____

_____

_____

_____

_____

_____

_____

_____

_____

_____

_____

_____

_____

_____

_____

_____

_____

_____

_____

_____

_____

_____

_____

_____

Date: **Day #**

Location:

Today: ☺   😐   ☹   😟   😠

Weather: ☀   ⛅   ☁   🌧   🌨

Notes

_____
_____
_____
_____
_____
_____
_____
_____
_____
_____
_____
_____
_____
_____
_____
_____
_____
_____
_____
_____
_____
_____
_____
_____
_____
_____

Date: Day #

Location:

Today: 🙂   😐   🙁   ☹️   😠

Weather: ☀️   ⛅   ☁️   🌧️   🌨️

Notes

Date: **Day #**

Location:

Today: ☺   😐   ☹   😕   😠

Weather: ☀   ⛅   ☁   🌧   🌨

Notes

Date: Day #

Location:

Today: ☺   😐   ☹   😖   😠

Weather: ☀   ⛅   ☁   🌧   🌨

Notes

Date: **Day #**

Location:

Today: 🙂 😐 🙁 😟 😠

Weather: ☀️ ⛅ ☁️ 🌧️ 🌨️

Notes

_____

_____

_____

_____

_____

_____

_____

_____

_____

_____

_____

_____

_____

_____

_____

_____

_____

_____

_____

_____

_____

_____

_____

_____

Sellos

Some sellos are inked heavily and may "bleed" through the page. Consider only applying sellos to only one side of the page to maintain the integrity of the stamp image.

Sellos

Sellos

Sellos

Sellos

Sellos

Sellos

Sellos

Sellos

Sellos

Sellos

Sellos

Sellos

Sellos

Sellos

Sellos

Sellos

Sellos

Sellos

Sellos

Sellos

Sellos

Sellos

Sellos

Sellos

Sellos

Sellos

Sellos

Sellos

Sellos

Sellos

Sellos

Sellos

Sellos

Sellos

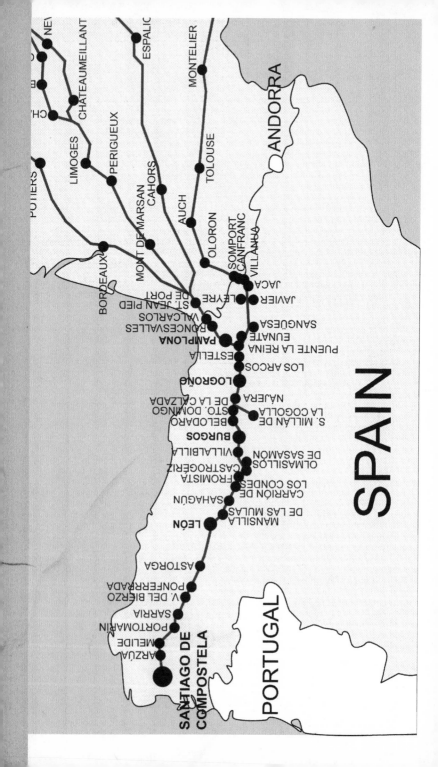

METRIC	STANDARD
1 centimeter	0.394 inch
1 meter	3.281 feet / 1.093 yards
1 kilometer	0.621 mile
1 gram	0.035 ounce
1 kilogram	2.205 pounds
1 milliliter	0.034 fluid ounce
1 liter	1.057 quart / 0.264 gallon

STANDARD	METRIC
1 inch	2.54 centimeters
1 foot	30.48 centimeters
1 yard	0.914 meter
1 mile	1.609 kilometers
1 ounce	28.350 grams
1 pound	454 grams / 0.454 kg
1 fluid ounce	29.574 milliliters
1 quart	0.946 liter
1 gallon	3.785 liters

°C	°F	°C	°F	°C	°F
0	32.0	13	55.4	26	78.8
1	33.8	14	57.2	27	80.6
2	35.6	15	59.0	28	82.4
3	37.4	16	60.8	29	84.3
4	39.2	17	62.6	30	86.0
5	41.0	18	64.4	31	87.8
6	42.8	19	66.2	32	89.6
7	44.6	20	68.0	33	91.4
8	46.4	21	69.8	34	93.2
9	48.2	22	71.6	35	95.0
10	50.0	23	73.4	36	96.8
11	51.8	24	75.2	37	98.6
12	53.6	25	77.0	38	100.4

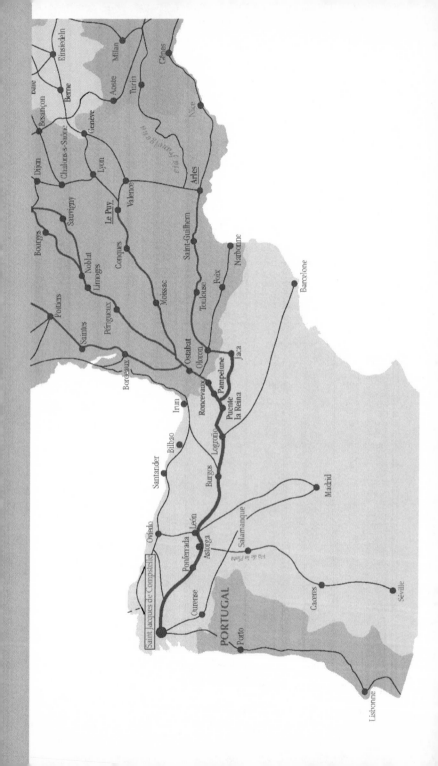